RICHARD LATOUR
Forward by Mark Leader

THE REAL ESTATE PYRAMID
An Agents Guide to Life on Top
By Richard Latour
Copyright © 2015

Published by:
Network Communications US Inc.
3057 Route 30, PO Box 580
Dorset Vermont, 05251
www.FreeFolders.com

Library of Congress Control Number: 2015951694

ISBN: 978-0-692-54897-4

All rights reserved. No part of this book may be reproduced or transmitted in any form or by any means, electronic or mechanical, including photocopying, recording or by any information storage and retrieval system, without written permission from the publisher, except for the inclusion of brief quotations in a review.

Forward

Early in my real estate career, which has evolved from sales to coaching, training, and speaking, I was told about this phenomenon called the Pareto Principle, or the 80-20 rule. In the late 1890s, Vilfredo Pareto discovered that 80 percent of the peas in his garden came from 20 percent of the pods, and also that 80 percent of the land in Italy was owned by 20 percent of the population. These discoveries and others came to inform his famous theory that for many events, 80 percent of the effects come from 20 percent of the causes. It's long been said that the Pareto Principle also applies uncannily to real estate agents and their production, with the top 20 percent handling the lion's share of the business.

So who are those 20-percenters, and what do they have that causes them to be the vital engines of the garden, the upper class, or the real estate industry?

Among all the real estate agents I've worked alongside, coached, mentored and trained over the years, I've found there is no inherent quality that separates the best from the rest. It doesn't matter if you're an introvert, extrovert, if you grew up wealthy or worked your way through high school. It doesn't matter if you're skilled with finance, marketing, or art; if you're a millennial or a baby boomer. People with all of these attributes are found among the 20 percent at the top.

Yet, while it isn't genetics or credentials, it also isn't luck that gets the 20-percenters there. There are some essential behaviors and attitudes that cause the most successful to surge ahead of all the rest. Richard Latour observed this phenomenon as well, and it inspired him to dig deeper and search for what, exactly, those behaviors were. As the co-founder of Network Communications, a company that creates folders for real estate agents featuring their business partners, he has the advantage not only of observing and talking with hundreds of agents, but also of making those observations from an outside perspective. It's a unique place to be. Latour's relationship with the real estate industry is close enough to smell the pines, but far enough to tell the forest from the trees.

Through Latour's eyes, you'll get an exclusive look into the lives and businesses of the top real estate agents. His stories are entertaining, conversational, and filled with insights you can use. If you're new to real estate, the lessons on the following pages will set you on the path to success.

The Real Estate Pyramid provides real-world examples of effective real estate branding, networking, and salesmanship behaviors. I know these behaviors work, because I see the results of teaching the same principles to my own students – things like finding an ownable niche within which you can develop your brand, staying in touch in meaningful ways with past clients, and using social media strategically.

In The Real Estate Pyramid, you'll read engaging stories of real agents who have overcome obstacles to success by sticking diligently to these behaviors. You'll also learn some things that might surprise you – like why the country club might not actually be the best place to network. Or why you should ignore the advice of certain veteran agents.

The 80-20 rule is still the reality of the real estate industry. But by following some simple rules of networking and sales, we can turn that pyramid upside down.

It all starts with knowledge – so read on.

I'll see you at the top.

Mark Leader, Founder, Leader's Choice Training and Coaching

Acknowledgements

First, I would to thank my dear wife Ann, my editor and best friend.

To Steve Dyball, my partner, friend, and Co-founder of Network Communications. The hardest working, and smartest sales manager that I have had the pleasure to work with in forty years of publishing.

Cheryl Malandrinos; real estate agent and copy editor. How fortunate for me that you wanted a folder. Helen Hossley of Vermont Realtors thanks for your insights and for pointing out the obvious. John Manfred of the Manfred Real Estate School the best friend an agent will ever have. Ted Adler founder of Union Street media, you continue to take real estate marketing to the next level. Mark Leader founder of Leaders Choice who identified the marks of a leader many years before I did, thank you for training the next generation of Super-agents.

Many thanks to the hundreds of collaborators on this book, the clients of Network Communications. It is your stories that makes my job interesting. Every week I discover another brilliant way that a real estate agent has turned an idea into a successful business. I never cease to be amazed by how practical, clever and creative you are. You cut through the clutter to see the obvious. You always manage to get the impossible done. Thank you for sharing your stories. I wish we could elect you all to a political office so we could get deals done in Washington. It is a fact, there is no one better equipped to negotiate compromises, than a successful real estate agent.

RL.

Preface - The Real Estate Pyramid

When I set out to use a metaphor for this book, the pyramid was the image that came to mind. Pyramids have thousands of stones at the base diminishing to just one at the top. They are built from the base up, an excellent comparison to a well-conceived real estate business. Or, so I thought.

To my surprise when you graph the income average for real estate agents, it starts out looking like a pyramid at the base, but gets thin in the middle. The high incomes at the top, averaged with the low ones at the bottom make the middle almost non-existent. Thus, a pyramid with no middle. It makes perfect sense, when you consider that the majority of real estate transactions involve only a small percentage of real estate agents. So I stuck with the pyramid image, but one with the middle removed. A good visual reminder to those who choose to sell real estate for a living.

Throughout the book, I cite case studies of clients with whom I have worked with over the years. In most cases, they would describe themselves as Brokers or Associate Brokers. Most are Realtors. For the sake of simplification and consistency, I describe them as real estate agents or agents. I have made changes in their descriptions. I did this to protect their identity and my client list. I have made the regions in which they work deliberately vague for the same reason. The central idea of this book is to give you both tolls and inspiration for your business. I consider the case studies to be its heart. We learn best from watching others.

Network Communications, the company that I co-founded, produces folders for real estate agents. What we do is to incorporate an agent's referral list into a presentation folder. It is free advertising for the agent, the folder is underwritten by the advertising.

The agent's client has all the resources necessary to complete a transaction, all in one place. We learned over time that the advertisers in the folders always refer real estate leads to these agents. The folder both defines and enhances that relationship.

It has been my extreme pleasure to work with many of the best real estate agents in the business. I have learned much from watching them work. These top agents share many of the same work habits and success is not accidental. I hope by sharing their stories, I can impart something of value to you, the reader.

Table of Contents

Forward - Some Thoughts Shared By Mark Leader - Leader's Choice.

Acknowledgements

Preface

Chapter 1: What Is The Real Estate Pyramid?	1
Chapter 2: Branding, Why Agents Brand Themselves.	5
Chapter 3: The Trinity Of Real Estate Networking.	13
Chapter 4: Past Client Networking.	17
Chapter 5: Professional Networking.	21
Chapter 6: Personal Networking.	27
Chapter 7: Your Networking Is Always Working.	33
Chapter 8: Social Media.	37
Chapter 9: Websites.	45
Chapter 10: What Is Your Real Estate Story?	51

About The Author 55

CHAPTER ONE

What is The Real Estate Pyramid?

Picture a pyramid with a small top, no middle and a very large base. That visual will help you understand the income profile of the real estate business. At the very top of the pyramid are the Super agents, the top one percent. The top producers control such a large percentage of the total transactions that they skew the average income for every other agent.

80% of Agents do 20% of the total transactions.

Eighty percent of real estate transactions are done by twenty percent of the agents. I refer to these agents throughout this book as the Twenty-percenters. If you are reading this, you may be working toward being part of that twenty percent. To achieve this, you will need to be clever, work hard, and have tremendous discipline. Statistically, the odds of success are long. Real estate sales is a business. A business where it is difficult to achieve success. But if you do succeed, it is a career you will truly love. A business where the rewards of success exceed most jobs. Obviously, there are different levels of expectations in real estate sales. A few want to be masters of the universe, a Super-agent, the top one percent. Many more will be happy doing a few transactions per year.

My friend John Manfred of the Manfred Real Estate learning center recently told me that 75 percent of the people taking his pre-licensing course will be out of the business in three years. He is currently expanding his program to teach people to sell real estate which is quite different than merely being legally eligible to do it.

There are as many reasons that people decide to sell real estate as there are real estate agents. A common theme among new agents is that you can choose your own hours and you have excellent earning potential. Other primary reasons are that it takes a minimal upfront investment to get started and it is relatively easy to get a job once you have your license. Let's separate the myths from reality.

Myth number 1. **A Comfortable Income.** Statistically, the average agent makes a respectable income, a comfortable middle class income. So a new agent might think a worse-case scenario is an average income. If this is what you are thinking, you should remember the pyramid has no middle. Eighty percent of real estate is sold by twenty percent of the agents. Which means that 80 percent of agents compete for the remaining 20 percent.

It is a small percentage of agents that make the statistically average income. They are usually the ones on the way to becoming a Twenty-percenter. The Twenty-percenters bring up the average income for everyone else. Among the twenty percent are the Super agents, the top one percent of the twenty percent. When you average Super agents exceptionally high incomes with everyone else you get the average. Remember, the Real Estate pyramid has a very small top, no middle and a very large base. It is the Twenty-percenters at the top. Everyone else is at the bottom.

Myth number 2. **You can set your own hours.** Agents work on straight commission, so indeed you do set your own hours. The Twenty-percenters work pretty much all of the time because that is what it takes to stay on top. As one recently told me, "If you are a Realtor, you are always on call. If you are not, someone else will be, it's more of a lifestyle than a job".

Real estate sales is not a job. It is a business. It takes discipline. It is competitive. Every person you come in contact with every day is a possible client or they may be a referral or a source of information. Set your hours, the hours totally devoted to building your business. Always remember that you are an agent, every minute of every day, always be looking for a lead. They always come when you least expect them. If you are not paying attention they never come at all.

Myth number 3. **You can work transaction to transaction or you can work by referral.** You sometimes hear descriptions of agents who work by transaction. Usually as an example of what not to do. There is no such thing as working by transaction, unless you have decided to become a permanent part of the base of the pyramid.

 If you want to be a Twenty-percenter, you will need to build your brand and a referral network. There are not enough hours in the week for you to prospect for clients, show property, list property and attend closings. It takes too much time to get everything accomplished and get to the closing table. If you want your business to exist at the top of the pyramid, you need to be working on multiple projects simultaneously. You need to learn how to network. It is the only way you will ever be a Twenty-percenter. These are the people you need to learn to compete with.

Twenty-percenters spend all their time working their referrals when they are not involved in a transaction. The key to becoming a Twenty-percenter or eventually a Super-agent is your success in building an effective referral network. You cannot advertise your way to success in real estate. You need to build your business from the ground up with effective branding and overlapping referral networks.

CHAPTER TWO

Branding - Why Brand Yourself?

If you don't think that branding is important, I would like to tell you the story of an advertising executive named Gary Dahl. In 1975 Gary was in a local pub drinking beer and listening to two friends complain about their pets. He immediately had an idea for a pet that didn't eat, get sick, need walks, and is easily trained. The pet rock.

The pet rock is an ordinary three inch gray stone that you can buy by the ton. He branded it "Pet Rock" and packaged it in a cleverly designed "Pet Carrier" sitting on straw. He included a manual containing information on how to care for your new pet. It suggested tricks that your pet could easily learn. Things like, by giving it a gentle nudge it will "roll over." Pet rocks are born with an innate ability to "stay" and to "play dead." Commands like "fetch" were difficult, but "attack" can be achieved with the assistance of the owner. Think about it.

The rocks cost a penny, the packaging and manuel around twenty five cents. During the six months they were available 1.5 million pet rocks were sold for $4.95. Gary became a millionaire. When is a rock not a rock? When it is branded as something else. Branding works.

During a recent visit to upstate New York, I noticed something interesting. In a one mile stretch there were four "Dollar" stores.

They were Family Dollar, Dollar General, The Dollar Store and Five Below where everything is priced between one and five dollars. All of these stores target the same customer, the discount shopper.

All of them sell an identical tube of Colgate toothpaste for essentially the same price. They all claim to have the lowest prices. The only way they differentiate themselves is through their branding. You, as an agent, offer the same exact service as every other agent. Branding is how you can differentiate yourself from the thousands of other agents in your market who perform the exact same service as you do.

In a survey done by the National Association of Realtors, 76 percent of people who decide to market their home interview only one agent. Essentially most have chosen their agent prior to the listing appointment. As an agent you are the product. This puts you in the unique position to decide how to present yourself to potential clients. The effort you put into your branding will increase your chances of being remembered by the right person at the right time. It will increase your chance of getting a listing or finding a buyer.

Branding for a real estate agent, as in other types of marketing, is most effective through repetition. It is generally accepted in print media that the content of an advertisement is only absorbed by the viewer after the third to sixth impression. So, if you ever wondered why you see the same advertisements over and over again, now you know. Real estate branding is a long term process. You must first decide what your focus will be. You will need to position yourself in your market and develop a long term plan.

Although you can make modifications along the way, the most effective branding varies little over time. It is difficult, once established, to modify your brand. A major change can take twice as long to accomplish as the establishment of a brand. In 1993 the rock musician "Prince" tried to change his professional name. He did this in order to get out of a contractual obligation with Warner Brothers records. In spite spending millions to accomplish recognition of his new name it was impossible to make the public understand. His album sold miserably. His contract expired, he took back his name and life went on. So it is important to look forward prior to starting. For instance, do you want to be a "foreclosure specialist" in a strong market with low unemployment? Do you want to be "The Condo Guy" in a market that is 77 percent single family homes? The answer might be yes if it means dominating a large enough segment, but you should take a long term view before committing to a brand that could limit your opportunities.

LinkedIn has 1.6 million registered users who describe themselves as real estate agents. Branding is the best way for you to distinguish yourself. It is a common practice among the Twenty-percenters. Agents do it because it works. Branding for real estate agents can be segmented into two categories: agent centric or business centric. Each category has its own strengths and weaknesses. Neither is perfect for everyone, but either is better than no branding at all.

Agent centric branding defines you as an agent. A Realtor from Texas goes everywhere in a Stetson Cowboy hat. He is pictured in all of his advertising wearing the hat. His signs include a graphic of the Hat. His photo appears in all of his advertising wearing the hat. His hat is his brand, he is referred to as the "Cowboy Realtor." He is easy to remember because of his hat. He has built his business around his brand.

There is an agent from Connecticut who calls herself the "Shoreline Homes Girl". She always dresses in pink and green. Her signs include a cartoon like picture of her dressed in pink and green. She uses that graphic in her ads, her note cards and it is at the bottom of every email she sends. When she recently changed Real estate agencies her brand went with her, and she never missed a beat. She has built a strong brand.

The advantages of agent centric branding is that you are easy to remember. If you use your branding wisely and understand search engine strategy, you can be easily found online. Someone need only remember how you brand yourself to find you. Your clients may even feel that they know you before you have met because of your branding. These are some of the strong positives of agent centric branding.

"For every action, there is a reaction." Unfortunately you cannot be all things to all people. What if a potential client dislikes cowboys? What if they do not take seriously a realtor who brands herself with a cartoon? Know your audience before you decide to go this route. The "Shoreline Homes Girl" wouldn't work too well in Austin, Texas. Nor would the cowboy be a smart choice on the Connecticut Shore.

Business centric branding focuses your business or market area. You might be a "new home specialist" or a "lakefront homes expert." You may refer to a region "I am your Hudson Valley Agent." Business centric branding can be effective, but it can also be limiting. The advantage to specific branding is it may give you the upper hand in your specialty. It may make you easier to find in a specific area during an online search.

It also has some obvious disadvantages. If you specify a region, what happens to possible listing outside of it? Can a "New Homes expert" list or sell an older home? Of course they can, but they might not get the chance. So be careful not to make your branding too specific. This type of branding is easier to modify than Agent Centric. Careful consideration here is advised.

Several years ago, we did a folder for a Super-agent from a bucolic New England town. Picture a Currier and Ives Christmas card. The houses are mostly late eighteenth and early nineteenth century colonials with Greek revival details. They are all painted white with green or black shutters. The antique lover's dream town. Not surprisingly, 65 percent of the housing stock are these old houses. The majority are owned and used as second or third summer or winter homes.

The Super-agent with whom I worked with branded herself as "A Historic and Antique home specialist." A smart choice for a town in which the majority of the housing stock falls into that category. She always leaves her house in a classic tailored outfit dressed and ready. Always looking like one of her toney clients. The way she looks and carries herself says "I have the same sensibilities as you" to her well healed clients. They trust her taste, she presents well, and she is her brand. She is so dominant in her category that the owners of these historic homes are reluctant to list with any other realtor. No matter what the "deal" is, and there is always a deal.

She recently sold a house to a couple from Connecticut. He is a Wall Street banker and she is a decorator. Their Connecticut residence is an early twentieth century architect designed Cotswold-Tudor mansion. It had been last updated not long after World War II. They oversaw a renovation that went to the studs and included a family room addition. The Banker was excited to do a similar project to an antique colonial home. They had come to the right place and had the right Realtor.

The Super-agent took them to view five properties that almost perfectly matched their criteria. These properties were listed in the 1.5 to 1.9 million price range. All had problems. The banker liked all of them, the decorator none. The decorator liked the details in these historic homes, moldings, fireplaces, paneled rooms etc. She didn't like the room proportions, layouts etc. She was worried about the time and effort it would take to renovate from a distance. There would certainly be hassles to create the house what she wanted.

The Super-agent used her mouth and ears proportionately. She listened twice as much as she talked. She knew that none of these houses could ever have modern room layouts because they were all in the town's historic district. Additions are difficult. No antique home would ever please the decorator. Luckily the Super-agent had an idea. She suggested they look at one more house that was not scheduled. It was eleven years old, not antique or historic, listed at 2.9 million. It was within the purchase and renovation budget of her clients. The Realtor suggested that it had great examples of the work of a local decorative painter, a great resource for them once they had found their dream home.

One quick tour of the property, a quick stop at the office to write the offer and the deal was done. It wasn't a historic antique they coveted. They actually wanted a beautifully finished home with central air they could move right in to. They just didn't know it. The Super-agent did because she listened. Throughout the day, the decorator had described what she wanted by telling the agent what she didn't want.

About a year later, the house next door to the banker sold. Friends of the banker came for a weekend visit and bought it. It was listed by the Super-agent. She got the listing because she had sold the home to the banker. The buyer was referred to the Super-agent by the banker. The Super-agent got the full commission on both sides of the transaction.

When we did a new folder for the Super-agent she made one change. She now brands herself "Antique and Significant homes". She continues to dominate the market. She continues to enjoy the view that living at the top of the pyramid affords her. She will do whatever it takes to stay there.

CHAPTER THREE

The Trinity of Real Estate Networking

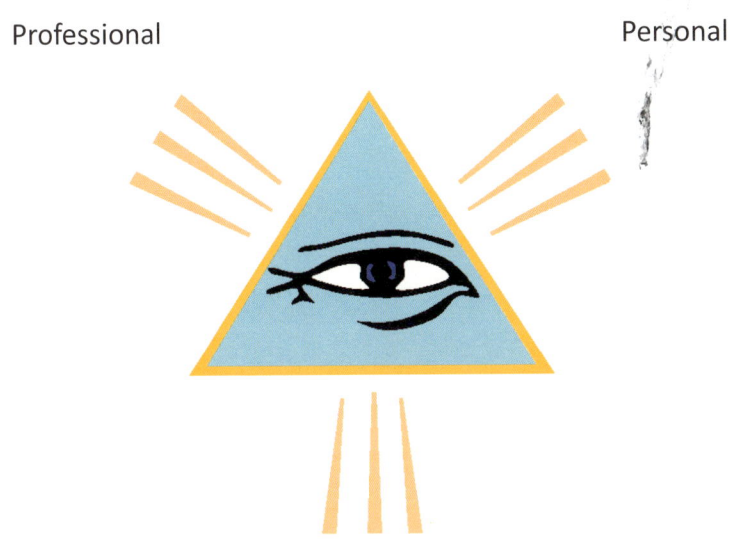

Professional Personal

Past Clients

Real Estate Networking can be sorted into three distinct groups I refer to them as the three P's. They are Past, Personal and Professional. I realize that many authors of networking books identify more than three categories, but I have consolidated them. The reason: these three networks all have a distinct manner in which an agent interacts with the people included. In many cases they overlap. In my personal experience at Network Communications, I have focused on the Professional category of real estate networking.

Before I move forward, I would like to remind you of the obvious. You don't interact with clients, businesses or associations. You network with people. People like to feel important. People like to be remembered. Twenty-percenters will often only have one thing in common, the ability to remember the names and details about virtually everyone they meet. You may assume it is a natural skill. It is not, it takes practice.

I once showed up without an appointment to the office of an agent who is listed amongst the top 100 in the United States. A Super-agent. You might refer to it as a drop-by. He remembered my name, where I was from, and he recalled the restaurant recommendation he gave me from my previous visit. He asked me if I had enjoyed the food. I was happy to tell him it was incredible and the service excellent. I have been back there several times.

Remember, the only other time we had ever met was when I was working on his folder. We had sat in his office and worked out a list of businesses that he refers clients to. These were the advertisers in his folder. During that time, he entered my name into his database, and he made notes on what we discussed that included the restaurant recommendation. After I left, he called the owner of the restaurant and let him know that I would be making a reservation. He gave the owner my name. Undoubtedly, he reminded the owner that he is always happy for a real estate referral. This is how to make a referral. This is how to become a Super-agent.

If he had not made note and called the restaurant, he undoubtedly would have forgotten the details. Those actions created a memory he was able to call upon even when I showed up unexpectedly. He did not need to refer to his database. Keep in mind that my visit had nothing to do with a current real estate transaction.

For a Twenty-percenter, networking is not something that is done only when they need new clients. For them it is a way of life, not a means to a short term goal. In the near term, you will not see measurable results, but over time you will notice an ever increasing number of your client's come through referrals.

Which agent would you assume the restaurant owner sends his referrals to? He is what I refer to as an advocate. Part of your job as an agent is to create advocates. The type of referral partner who is always on the lookout for a client for you. If you do this you will eventually be dining at the top of the pyramid. The food there is excellent.

CHAPTER FOUR

Past Clients

Past Clients - Look Forward With One Eye In Your Rearview Mirror

Depending on who you believe, the average homeowner stays in their home about ten years and a condo owner about seven. Both numbers have been trending down since 2003. A previous customer is a potential new client provided you understand the horizon. Things happen, people move, you never know. Remember ten years is an average, and like the real estate pyramid, average might not mean that much. You need to stay in touch with your previous clients. You need to be remembered.

You should always keep in mind, that no matter how well you do your job, your clients do not owe you a referral. In fact, they won't refer you unless you keep in touch with them and ask them to. Your past clients are experts on your service as an agent. A referral from them is worth more than from any other lead source. Their first-hand experience with you can be relayed without prejudice.

It is generally accepted that a satisfied client will tell one person about you. An unsatisfied customer will tell six. Think about that. An unsatisfied customer can set you back big time. Your customers believe that you make a ton of money in commissions. They have absolutely no idea how hard it is to do what you do, and many may think that you are overpaid. The most important thing to learn as an agent is how to manage your client's expectations.

What you want to do is to turn your customers into advocates. Bring your clients a closing gift, something unique, something that will last. I often see Cutco knives exhibiting at real estate conferences. They sell knives to agents with your name engraved on them. Remember the ten year average. Give your clients something they will use every day and that will last ten years.

If the house next door to the one you sold goes for less, let your client know. People are naturally curious about home prices. If you have a story to tell, by all means tell it. Keep in touch after the sale and stay interested. Agents who take networking courses are always asking for referrals. It is printed on their cards, notes and emails. "I am never too busy for your referrals." I would certainly encourage this. But give your clients a reason to refer you; remind them of who you are. Be excellent at what you do. Build a referral base of satisfied customers and never neglect it. It is your most important asset. Your past clients should be part of your real estate business.

I recently worked on a folder for an upstate Twenty-percenter, a former Super-agent. His office walls are covered with golf pin flags; his credenza is covered with trophies. He is a seriously good golfer. The area he covers has two strong and distinct demographics. A large upper middle class base and a smaller group of wealthy professionals and business owners.

When he was a Super-agent he built a referral network from past clients that was almost not to be believed. Entirely among the larger upper middle class group. In a cul-de-sac that contained eight custom built colonials, he sold five. All in an eighteen month period, four were referrals from previous customers. He would take his clients to the local municipal golf course where he would be introduced to more clients. He was working, even when he wasn't working. He had six different overlapping referral networks that were all feeding him leads at the same time. His office ran like a well-oiled, lead generating machine.

He is a seriously nice guy who became seriously wealthy. Because of his golf prowess, he was invited to play in the member-guest tournament at the local Country Club. A club with a course designed by a famous golf architect, with a fabulous clubhouse which is immaculately maintained. The kind of place that cost a fortune. After winning the tournament his member friend suggested that he join the club. He was in heaven. He was put up and seconded for membership and his application immediately approved. All of his friends, past clients and everyone who knows him were very happy for him. He had made it big, and everyone felt he deserved it. He did deserve it.

Pretty soon, he became absorbed in club activities, playing golf there every weekend, attending dinners and parties. His business began to shrink from its highs, but he maintained a respectable income. It went on that way for about a year, until 2008 when the bottom dropped out of the real estate market.
That is when he decided to go back to the basics. He began to contact his former clients. Many hadn't heard from him in two years or more. Many had formed loyalties with other realtors. One was surprised to hear from him, she had assumed he had retired, yipe that hurt. Poor market conditions combined with three years of neglect had taken its toll. The business he built up over thirteen years had seriously diminished. The momentum was gone.

Three years ago, he resigned from his club. It's not because he could no longer afford it. He just decided that it was too much of a distraction. He is now playing golf again at the municipal course. He invited me to play with him. He reminded me that if I ever hear about anyone moving to the area he is never too busy to handle a referral. He has once again built a strong business. He is a Twenty-percenter on his way to regaining his Super-agent status. It like the old adage "Give a man a fish and he will eat for a day; teach him to fish and he will eat for a lifetime." It is more important to know how to build a real estate business than it is to sell a house.

Before I left his office I asked him what he learned from it all. He said "Don't forget to dance with the one who took you to the party." I think that is pretty good advice for a real estate agent. It made me wish I had a referral for him. Always remember that the real estate pyramid has no middle, there is nothing holding you up at the top. But if you keep in touch with your past clients, they just might be willing to help.

CHAPTER FIVE

Professional Networking - The Closest Thing To A Sure Thing

On average, a real estate transaction generates over 25,000 dollars in economic activity. Real estate agents are the single most important referral source to this revenue. It is essential that you make the most of your referrals to these vendors. Referrals should be mutual.

Networking with Businesses in real estate is quite different from the other two types of networking. Agents cannot get to a closing without the help of as many as twenty other people in some transactions. These people can be virtual gold mines as referral partners to you, if they are handled correctly.

This may seem obvious, but the only reason a business refers business to you as a realtor is that they expect you to reciprocate. If you want to continue to get referrals from these people, you must return the favor. A simple thank you note will not cut it here.

When referring a business, it is absolutely essential that they know the referral came from you. If you know your client is going to use one of your partners do not send them an email. Emails go unread, overlooked and they have no shelf life. Use your personal note cards to let your partner know that the referral came from you. A note card will be opened. A note card might stick around their office for a few weeks, serving as a constant reminder of your referral. You can be certain that if your partners collect a few of your note cards, you will come to mind when the times comes. Refer to these people as your partners when talking to them.
All business referrals are not created equally. Let me explain. The Professional networking group is split into two categories. First

there is the transaction category. This includes anyone who is involved in the normal transaction of real estate. It is important to know the laws regarding referrals in your state. Many states require multiple referrals in certain categories.

- Closing Attorneys (or title companies in the States that use them to close transactions)
- Banks or Mortgage Lenders
- Home Inspectors
- Insurance Agencies

In the transaction related category it is important to remember that these people work with multiple agents. The real estate market is essentially their only source of business. They live on these transactions. It can be difficult for them to refer clients, to one realtor exclusively. It can take a lot of time to figure out who your partners are in this category. If you are currently getting referrals from lenders for pre-approved clients, you know how hard that was to accomplish. Never take it for granted. A referral among this group is almost always a "thank you" for your referral.

The broader group of professionals is the home improvement section. These people interact with your clients in two ways. First, a home inspector will identify a situation in a home that is a safety issue or that impacts value. A professional electrical contractor, roofer, plumber etc. will be brought in to give an estimate for a repair. The repair becomes part of the negotiation and regardless of how it gets paid for, the work gets done. The contractor brought in has an advantage in getting the work. They will not forget who brought them in. Here again is a good use for your note cards.

The professionals in the improvement section are not solely dependent on real estate transactions as a source for business. This gives them the ability to be more loyal to an agent who regularly refers business to them. When deciding which of these professionals to network with, I would make two suggestions. First, make a list of fair and competent people. You should never refer a client to someone overpriced or under qualified. It reflects poorly on you as an agent. Second, which of these people would refer business to you? Pick the ones that you are most certain of. That is how to develop your referral list.

We once did a folder for an agent who included an auto repair shop on his referral partner list. The Realtor had been sending clients to him for years and he was certain he would want to advertise. When we called on the owner of the shop, he was not interested in advertising. He mentioned another realtor in the area and said if we did a folder for her, he would be very interested. It turns out that the owner's niece worked for this competing realtor. He was referring business to her. The agent we were working with appreciated this information.

The list below is a suggestion of professionals you should include on the improvement section of your referral list. It is important that you know the laws of your state when it comes to making referrals. Many states require to make multiple referrals in certain categories.

- Alarms/Locksmith
- Pest Control
- Heating/AC
- Plumbing
- Electrical
- Chimney Sweep
- Excavation
- Home Repair

- Home Builder
- Septic
- Landscaper/maintenance
- Carpet Cleaning
- Handy man
- Carpenter
- Builder
- Caretaker
- House painter

We recently did a networking folder for an agent who listed a house painter on her referral list. We sold the entire folder out quickly, she is a Super-agent. Virtually everyone we contacted wanted to be included on this folder. Before we went to print we shared the advertisers list with the agent.

She sent me a one line terse e-mail asking me to contact her. She wanted to know why her painter was not on the advertiser list. I explained we had tried but were unable to contact him, and we had no more space in her folder. She insisted we make space and that she would contact him. Within an hour we received a call from him on his cell phone from Florida. He spends his winters there. He, of course, wanted to be in the folder, and we made space for him. It is impossible to say no to a Super-agent.

She later explained to me that her relationship with the painter went all the way back to when she got her Real Estate license. Over the years they had referred dozens of clients to each other. Most recently the painter had been called in to do several rooms of a 2.5 million dollar lakefront home by the children of its owner.

Their mother had been recently moved to a nursing home. They were planning to put the home on the market and had not decided on whom to list it. The painter suggested our Super-agent client. She got the listing and eventually the buyer of the house. Do the math, she is the owner/broker with a full commission on both sides of the transaction. You can't always put a value on a referral, but you certainly could on this one.

Networking with businesses, especially those that cater to real estate, will extend your reach. A referral from these partners often converts into a potential client. Having these partners in the field can put you in the right place at the right time. Climbing to the top a pyramid takes work. You need all of the help you can get.

CHAPTER SIX

The Real Estate Pyramid - Personal Networks

Real Estate sales is all about timing. You need to be in the right place at the moment in time when a potential client is ready to buy or sell. You cannot be everywhere at the same time, but you can achieve this result through surrogates. You need scouts. The way to accomplish this by utilizing your personal networks. An agent, properly networked, has the ability to be everywhere always. You must come to mind when people hear about real estate. The most memorable thing about you should be that you are an agent. That you can get the deal done. Your personal networks should be advocates for your real estate business. It is the most common trait of a Twenty-percenter.

All though personal networks can be the least reliable networking source, they have the potential to be the most far reaching. In professional networking you are limited by the number of people you refer business to. When networking with past clients, that number is limited to your transaction count. Your personal networks include everyone that you have ever been in contact with no matter what the context. Your personal networks will change over time but a smart agent will stay connected to as many as possible. They will change and grow as time goes on.

I recently had the occasion to work with an agent from the suburbs. She had an interesting real estate story that illustrates the changing nature of personal networks. After college she moved to a major East Coast city with the idea to pursue a career in women's fashion. She was accepted into the training program of a major retailer where she proceeded to work seven days a week as an assistant buyer. She was making just enough money to cover her school loans, rent, and food. She had little time for fun. By her sixth month she realized that her dream job had turned out to be a nightmare. After some soul searching, she quit.

She spent the next three weeks looking all day, every day, for something else to do. She was facing the prospect of moving home with her parents and in all likelihood, saying good bye to her new boyfriend. Out of sheer desperation she took a part time job as a receptionist at an upscale real estate agency. The kind of place where her stylish wardrobe made her a natural fit. Over the next several months, she began to learn more about what went on there.

Her first impression of the agents there was that their phones seemed permanently connected to their heads. The more successful ones rarely came to the office and had little patience for anything that went wrong. They spent their entire day talking to people, never taking their eyes off their phones. They spoke well, dressed better, and only addressed the immediate task at hand. They were completely immersed in the various deals they were working on, in different stages all at once.

A recently married college friend called her at home one day; she was hoping to buy a co-op. Her friend knew she was working in real estate and was looking for an agent. She immediately referred her friend to an agent who had several listings in the right neighborhood, and who seemed to have an interest in her. Her friend eventually bought a co-op based on that referral.

Two days after the closing, she found an envelope from the agent who sold the co-op. It contained a check for one thousand dollars. The note said, "Thank you for the referral, you should really get your license. You would be good at this and I don't say this to everyone."

Within a few months she took her licensing exam and became an agent. She began calling all of her college friends in high priced rentals and explained the advantages of owning. She visited with all of her fashion friends and reminded them when the timing was right she was there to help. Her biggest windfall came when she began to help out her now husband's financial services friends with their real estate needs. She became an expert in "starter apartments." As time went on "larger apartments." After the birth of her first son in "apartments near good schools." Within a few years she built a very successful business. Everything was on track, the future predictable. Until one day, two planes flew into the World Trade Center.

Now pregnant with her second son, she moved to the suburbs. Not yet licensed in her new state, she continued to work on deals until the two hour commute made it untenable. Three months after the birth of boy number two she became pregnant with boy number three, "Irish twins". With three under the age of five, she gave up real estate entirely. Or so she thought.

Micro-soccer is an event that young mothers go to with their barely walking children. A ball, which appears to have magnetic qualities, is placed on a field where it is immediately surrounded by wildly flailing young soccer stars. The parents use this diversion to discuss the topics of the day. A common topic being the inadequacies of their current home.

Our client now drives a Honda minivan which has a pair of soccer balls hanging from the rearview mirror. This unintended sculpture might be an unconscious reminder of how far her journey has come from her career in women's fashion. Over the past ten years she has built up a real estate business networking with the soccer moms and others she has met from any other activity connected with her children. She often spends her entire day in her yoga clothes and confesses to "only occasionally wearing make-up." She never stops talking about real estate and during our meeting, reminded me three times that my referrals would have her full attention. She told me how many transactions she closed last year; this soccer mom is a Twenty-percenter. Although the top of the pyramid may be small there is plenty of room for you, and your children.

We recently did a folder for a Super-agent who I heard about through a closing attorney who has advertised in several of our folders. I immediately contacted her and met with her to work on her referral list. She had recently become an associate broker and was about to celebrate her fourth year selling real estate. I was completely blown away by her. She had 36 featured listings on her personal website. She had 16.5 million dollars in sales the previous year in a market where the average home sells for 300,000 dollars. She built her entire business in four years, with no previous sales experience. It almost seemed impossible.

In her recent past life, she had been a nurse. She was used to working long hours and is extremely organized. She loved being a nurse but the outcomes on the cardiac ward were often upsetting to her. During the process of buying a new home she decided to become an agent. Remember, this nurse is now a multi-million-dollar producer.

Upon getting her license she immediately contacted everyone she ever knew from her previous life. She explained that she was going to specialize in finding convenient, affordable homes for medical professionals. She offered a small discount on her commission to these people. She branded herself as the agent who understands their special requirements. She reminded them she was one of them.

She began to get referrals through her colleagues for nurses and doctors moving in and out from both hospitals where she had worked. Just prior to our meeting she had signed a listing with a woman who had practically begged her to take it because it was near the hospital. This woman did not believe any other agent could to sell her house. She wanted a specialist. As her business grew, she began to rely less on her past. When she sold a million-dollar home to a doctor she canvased the neighbors to let them know if they decided to sell, she had the clients.

Soon, she just became well known and an agent who gets deals done.

She is an example of effective branding and working by referral. She has never spent a single dollar on any type of advertising, yet she lives at the top of the Real Estate Pyramid

CHAPTER SEVEN

Rule 1. Your networking is always working

Rule 2. When your networking is not working refer to Rule 1

Never assume your efforts will go unrewarded. For several years, I did folders on a large lake in New England. I did them for virtually every Real Estate agency on the lake. I also do folders at all of the nearby lakes in the region, virtually every office. These agents like our folders because they are branded for the area and for their offices. There is a strong second home market in part, because the weekly rental market for lake houses is strong.

The agents use our folders to deliver rental receipts and keys to the houses. They often enclose a "things to do" package including a map of the area. People who rent these lake homes often become buyers. The folders remind the renter of the agent they used. Secondly, if they become buyers, the advertising includes all of the resources to complete a transaction. Finally, when people drop into the office to grab a real estate magazine or general information, it is delivered in a folder. Folders have a lot more presence than a business card; they may get tossed but they won't get lost.

I was never able to get an appointment with the owner of the largest, most prestigious office in the area. A multiple office agency, it is owned by a second generation agent who inherited the business from his father. It was always my assumption that because he hadn't started the business, he was a hands off manager. That if he was actually selling homes, he would want our folders. No matter how hard I tried I could not get his attention. I will even admit to stalking his office in hopes of "running in to him" on his way to his car. This strategy might sound all too familiar to some of more experienced readers.

One afternoon, the phone rang. The caller ID indicated it was from his office. Since he had never responded to me before, I assumed he was calling to ask to be removed from our mailing list. Instead, he asked me some questions and gave me an appointment. After he hung up, I went onto his web site. He had twice as many listings as any of his agents. He was not a manager; he was a Super-agent. He had gotten all of my mailings, emails and phone messages over the past few years. I had been mentioned to him by several businesses we network with. He wasn't ignoring me, he was just busy.

The reality is that the most important thing he inherited from his father was networking skills and a work ethic. When we sold the advertising in his folder, everyone we contacted considered him a personal friend. He is never in his office because he spends all of his time networking with past clients and their caretakers, with every contractor and every association, group, and business on the lake. When we met to do his referral list, it was already on his computer; it consumed seven pages.

The bigger the effort, the bigger the reward. Always assume your networking is working, sometimes it just takes time.

I recently met with a broker that we created a folder for three years earlier. She was in the process of opening a second office about thirty miles from her first one. She wanted a folder that contained the referral partners of the agents who would be using it. She understood that branding is not the sole purpose of a folder, that networking is what makes it effective. She wanted to be sure that her agents will succeed. The folder had to contain the right people, their people.

In her previous life she had been a clinical social worker. She eventually became the Executive Director of an alliance that represented 25,000 members. She would spend the better part of each week traveling throughout the state meeting with members and attending conferences. It was a grueling schedule. She loved it and it worked for her until the unexpected happened, her mother became terminally ill. She retired, and spent the next year taking care of her mother. She reflected on how she wanted to spend the rest of her life.

She had always been good with people and good at sales. As a girl she broke every record for selling girl-scout cookies. As an adult, a sales director for Mary Kay cosmetics. She knew she had sales skill, organizational ability and determination to succeed. The only question unanswered was at what?

She relied on two friends for advice. The first had spent several years selling real estate, all of them during the boom that abruptly ended in 2008. She worked from transaction to transaction and unfortunately spent almost no time building her business. She did not refer clients to people who might be inclined to reciprocate. She did not keep in touch with her past clients. She practically kept her profession a secret from everyone she met. During the course of four years she passed out less than 200 business cards. In spite of this she earned a fairly good living for a time, until it all ended. She cautioned her friend against going into real estate. Her second friend, a lawyer, was selling property part-time while building up her law practice. In most states, passing the bar, is the only requirement for selling houses. She encouraged our client to do it. She understood the potential, and the up-front investment is pennies on the dollar compared to getting a law degree. She convinced her friend to go into real estate.

She attended classes at the Manfred Real Estate School in New

York and passed her licensing exam. She got a job with a local real estate office, but with no training was having trouble succeeding. After several months she moved to a bigger office but had the same results. It turns out that being qualified to sell real estate and knowing how to do it are two entirely separate things.

She went back to school and took an intensive course form a well-respected real estate trainer. She wanted to be proactive not reactive in her profession. She learned how to schedule her day in a way that utilized the hours not related to transactions to building her business. She created a referral list, a past clients and personal database. At first she used the course material like a menu. She would pick and choose what she would incorporate into her business. As she used it more, and trust the results, she realized it is a system with everything working together. She began to use it the way it is designed to work.

She now has the licenses of nine agents hanging on the wall of her office. She has her own networking group that meets for coffee and doughnuts the first Wednesday of every month, the members share leads and information with each other. Every mother's day she drives around delivering flowers to her past clients that she buys from the florist in her network. She averages around thirty listings and sells them faster than any other agent in her board. She was not the quickest agent that I ever witnessed ascend to the top of the pyramid but her being there is no accident. It never is. She will undoubtedly be breathing the clear air up there for a long time to come. The systems that she built her business on will practically insure it.

CHAPTER EIGHT

Branding and Networking using Social Media

As I noted earlier, 76 % of home owners interview only one agent prior to listing their home. This statistic illustrates why the pyramid has no middle. Listings go to relatively few agents. The competition for them is over before it starts. Equally important is the fact that virtually every new home buyer finds their home online. If you intend to find a life at the top of the pyramid, you need to understand the web. Effective use of social media is no longer an option, it is a requirement. The importance of digital market continues to grow as more millennials enter the real estate market. They live in an almost entirely digital world.

Planning is the key to a successful social media strategy. It is your vision that is the key to a successful plan. Before you start a strategic plan for your social media strategy, you must analyze your business. Your social media presence should be an extension of your brand. Your followers should include your entire network. If you don't have a clear starting point and an equally clear destination, you will struggle. Your results should be measurable. Your time is too valuable to invest in something that does not bring results.

Once you figure out how you want to present yourself you can implement a social media strategy.. You should have both short and long term goals. In the short term:

1) Determine which platforms to use. This is your starting point.

Choose the social media communities that you want your business to engage with. Each social media platform has its own distinct demographic and atmosphere; choose which ones best suit your brand and potential customer base. What kind of content do you want to produce? Twitter is short form text content while Facebook, Pinterest, Instagram, and YouTube are better for visual content. Think about who your audience is and where they reside online. Facebook has become popular among older buyers, while your younger clients gravitate toward Twitter. Ask your clients what they use. Evaluate your business and decide, where is the most effective place to put your message?

2) Research your competitors.

After you choose your social media platforms, scan them for your competitors. What are they doing? Do they have good or poor engagement from their followers? Make a note of which strategies work for them and which strategies you can use to your advantage. Use these platforms to enhance your brand. Evaluate which posts draw a reaction from your base.

3) Grow your fan base.

No matter what the platform experiment with search terms relevant to your market. What combinations will take them to you? In turn, optimize your own page with keywords like "real estate" so that people can find you when they conduct their own searches. Include your state and town in your content. These techniques help you to build a targeted community for your business.

You can also leverage social media ads to put your brand in front of an even larger community. Both Twitter and Facebook are excellent places to share information about your new listings. Original content is most desirable. You should prioritize your choice of social media based on your business and your message, each has a unique focus, strength and weakness. I have listed below the platforms that are useful to marketing real estate.

Facebook

Facebook is an online social networking site that allows its users to create personal profiles, add other users as friends and interact with other users through personal messages and public wall posts. People can also post status updates and photos directly to their profile. Facebook is a great place to start for real estate agents who want to increase their online presence since it offers targeted ad strategies and an intuitive analytics dashboard for business pages. Facebook also offers access to a huge audience (the company has 1.28 billion users). Approximately 65% of its users are age 35 older. The perfect target for your more expensive homes.

Twitter

Twitter is a platform that allows its users to interact with 140-character posts called "tweets." It's often referred to as the "SMS of the Internet" and has roughly 255 million users. The site handles millions of tweets and almost two billion search queries per day. Twitter allows businesses to purchase ad space with promoted tweets and lead generation cards, as well as a free analytics dashboard at analytics.twitter.com. Twitter was ranked as one of the 10 most visited websites of 2013.

Google+

Google+ is a social media site created by Google. The interesting aspect of Google+ is that it not only functions as a networking site; content posted on your Google+ account can be associated with your site and enhance your authority in search engine rankings. The site has approximately 540 million users, making it the second-largest social media site behind Facebook.

LinkedIn

LinkedIn is a social networking service specifically designed around professional networking. Therefore, it offers a unique advantage for real estate agents who want to network with other Realtors and boost their industry knowledge. 1.6 million LinkedIn subscribers identify themselves as real estate agents. LinkedIn allows both personal and company pages to create profiles on the site and interact with other users. People can build online groups and forums with LinkedIn to discuss industry news; real estate agents often join discussion groups to stay updated on local and national market trends. The site has approximately 300 million users.

YouTube

YouTube is a video-sharing social media site owned by Google. Users can create accounts on the site to upload, view, and share videos. People can also comment on videos and interact with other users on comment threads. The site offers a real advantage to real estate agents who want to promote video blogs or clips of house tours. These videos can be linked to your website.

Instagram

Instagram is a social networking site where people can upload, share, and comment on short videos and photos. The site allows users to apply digital filters to their pictures and share those photos across other sites like Facebook and Twitter. Real estate companies could see some benefit from this site by posting photos of new listings and local attractions. Instagram offers access to a younger demographic – especially the sought-after market of millennials; 90% of its 150 million users are under the age of 35.

Pinterest

Pinterest is a social media site based on the idea of discovery. Users can create collections – also known "boards" – of "pins" that detail everything from DIY projects to dinner recipes. The site has about 70 million largely female users and analysts speculate that ads on the site could generate up to $500 million in 2016. Real estate agents who use Pinterest often create boards for new listings, DIY advice, and local attractions. Buyers are more likely to use this social media site when looking for a new house, and they will likely curate boards of listings in their desired location.

Once you have chosen your platforms, begin to accomplish your social media goals.

1) Be consistent in your messaging.

Your web presence should be an extension of your business. Reinforcing your brand is the most important thing you do every day. Repetition is the mantra of effective branding. What will make you stand out?

What is the essential message of your company? What do you want your clients to know about you? If you're an agent that wants to be known as an expert in land transactions, consider building your social media posts around questions and news concerning land transactions. Share your success stories with your audience as well as your listings. Social media tells the ongoing story of you as a real estate agent. If you think of it this way, what would you want people to remember about you?

2) Find industry thought leaders.

Just like searching for potential clients online, you can also search for experts in your field. These experts will provide you with valuable content that you can share with your followers. Consider following pages like Inman News (@InmanNews) to find content for your social media pages. Always make it relevant to your local area. Try to make it personal.

3) Discover ways to recycle content across platforms.

Share content from your blog or website on your social media platforms. This content provides value to your followers and also encourages them to visit your website. Introduce your new listings and announce recent sales. Social media should be proactive.

4) Learn to write for the web.

Much of your content will require original writing. It is a delicate balance to satisfy human visitors as well as search engines. Don't write spam in the hopes of enhancing your search results. Google and Bing can see right through the endless repetition of key words. Your clients will search for something more interesting to read. Remember that every page is a potential landing site from a search engine. They should all have a coherent theme. Your text should always include a call to action. Every page should include a visible link to your contact page as well as your phone number.

5) Format your content.

It really doesn't matter how good your content is if nobody reads it. Large blocks of text should be avoided, your reader will quickly navigate away from it. The use of headings will facilitate the sectioning of an ideas and keep the text manageable. This will also help the search engines understand your topic. Use images to illustrate your content, but be mindful, they do nothing to enhance search results. 250 words is a good minimum target. It is long enough for the search engines to get your idea. When writing for the web, less is more.

6) Publish, test, and repeat.

Once you have a few solid social media posts under your belt, figure out what resonates best with your audience. Platforms like Facebook and Pinterest have analytic features that observe and document how people engage with your posts. Do you get more likes and views on posts with pictures? Posts that use humor? Once you find your best content, continue to use the same strategies to build engagement of your brand.

Every successful social media strategy requires a bit of trial and error. Be patient with yourself and your company, stay diligent with your posts, and watch how your social media presence can drive your business.

CHAPTER NINE

Websites

Your First Impression or Not?

In 2008 I spent a week in the home office of the fastest growing real estate agency in New England. The company was founded in 2003 by a former telecommunications executive who recognized the potential of the internet for the real estate business. His concept was simple, develop an optimized website that will always come up first on organic home searches. He would then point the client to the agent who had the listing, as long as it was his agent. If it wasn't, he would send the lead to an agent who was. He could effectively double the commission of a listing agent by sending them a buyer. A pretty compelling recruitment tool.

His business partners were computer programmers, and they understood the algorithms of the search engines. His website was designed to capitalize on that knowledge. In five years he had recruited over 100 agents and he was operating out of eight offices. He would bring in a potential agent and have them search for property in their town. No matter what key words were used, he was always listed in the top spot. I was creating networking folders for all eight of his offices; he now has fourteen offices and over 300 agents.

His rapid growth alerted many other real estate professionals in his market to the power of the internet. I asked Ted Adler, the founder of Union Street Media, about this phenomenon, as his company specializes in real estate website development and digital marketing. His reply was that the Bean Group stepped up the quality of sites throughout New England. In the 21st century, if you do not have an effective website you can no longer exist in the real estate business. Real estate agents and brokers sought out companies like Union Street Media to help compete.. Today over ninety-nine percent of home buyers see their home first online. On their computers, phones or tablets.

Your website can be your most important asset. It should be a continuation of your brand as well as effective in drawing traffic, balancing the art of your brand with the science behind search engines. A graphically pleasing website is great as long as it gets found, but it really doesn't matter how good it looks if nobody sees it. Search engine algorithms change constantly and the optimization process never ends. Your website must have the capability to search the MLS "integrated": framed solutions or links to third party websites where the data may appear to be on your domain name, but is not, will significantly impact your ability to rank well. If your site does not provide a good user experience and relevant data, your client will jump to a website that does. You need to keep your clients searching on your site. Your website is essential to your success.

No amount of advertising on Trulia, Realtor.com or Zillow will work for you if you do not have an effective landing site for your potential customers. If your listing is found online, your prospective client will likely contact you that way. Your website is that connection. It is vitally important to pick a web provider that specializes in web development and digital marketing for the real estate industry as they will be able to provide real estate specific software and site functionality that a generalist will not. To a client who doesn't know you, your website is you!

Design is an important element in website development. In the past, many agents created animated, flash-heavy websites to dazzle visitors. Today, developers believe that flash heavy websites daze and confuse consumers. People are more sophisticated at searching for websites thanks to companies like Google. However, the "user experience" is about more than balancing design and search engine optimization strategies. Website design is about structure. According to Union Street Media's Vice President of Product, John Merse, "There is a step in the web design process known as Information Architecture. IA is the development of the web site's structure and navigation. This framework or "wire frame" provides a map of the content and functionality that will drive the design and development process and result in the finished website." Think about the design structure and layout of your site like an architect would about designing a new home. The questions raised before actually building a home are very similar to those a developer will ask before building your website.

Understanding your audience will help determine the look and feel of your website. Your builders should understand your market and your business before starting the project. What types of properties do you typically list? What is the prevalent architecture in your community? The images on your website should look like the area you serve. Who are your intended buyers? What do you want people to remember about you?

It's important that you also understand how the design of your site will influence your ability to be found. Flash and image heavy websites tend to have a harder time in the rankings. Remember, Google is a text matching engine: it needs to be able to read content on your website, which should be unique to your site and specific to your area. A great web site design will deftly balance all of these elements, increasing your chances of being found amid the sea of other real estate web sites. Is your built on a content management system that enables you to easily add and update content? Are your newest listings automatically fed into your site once you enter them into the MLS? Google also prefers sites that have regularly updated content. Adding a blog to your domain and creating unique content are two of the easiest ways to help your search results. Keep in mind that prospective seller will start checking your website before you leave their driveway too, so your site content should be addressed to more than just buyers.

Understanding how customers use your site will help you understand what needs updating, it will also help to increase your leads. Your site is a portal for customers to view properties and find out if you are the right agent for them. Some clients will also want information regarding the communities they are thinking about moving to or information on relocating to a new area. Especially for new buyers, recommending specific searches that buyers can access in one click is a great way to showcase real estate in your area. As a fringe benefit, search engines love links to recommended searches.

The design of your website should be simple, easy to view and navigate. The links should be obvious. If you are having trouble making a decision about a button or content, remember that the simplest answer is often best. Also, make sure the font on your site is large enough so all visitors can easily read it—including users with small, old screens and weaker reading vision. It should appeal to a broad audience with varying degrees of computer skills, and it must to be compatible with phones and tablets.

Remember, you are not only competing against other agents in your market, you are competing against other markets. So, a web site for Cape Cod should make you want to buy a beach house there. There is an old sales proverb that applies here: if you are selling Caribbean beach vacations, you should describe the feeling of sand between your toes while walking on the beach. In addition to the first impression, a site infused with local imagery helps show buyers that you are passionate and knowledgeable about your area. Make your site appealing, insure that your client's want to come back to visit you again. Remember, you are in the dream business.

A website that doesn't brand you is not as effective as it should be. Your website should distinguish you from your completion and be an extension of everything else you do. Your brand should be consistent across all your marketing platforms: website, lawn signs, print advertising etc. You wouldn't create a road sign that can't be read by a driver going 50 miles per hour. The same thinking should be used when designing your website. A user should know they are on your site with just a quick glance, before they start reading content. That is what makes effective branding. Simpler is better. It is no accident that Warren Buffet chose to use the Berkshire Hathaway name when he decided to get into the real estate business. He has been in business since 1955 and his brand is well respected. Whether he is successful or not will be determined over time. "Berkshire Hathaway" is his home field advantage. What is yours? Incorporate it in your website.

Many agents have their referral partners listed on their websites. It can be an excellent place to extend your network. Whether you do or not is a matter of preference. Some agents feel it might prevent someone not listed from referring them. Others feel that it creates loyalty from the people listed. In the end it depends on your business, community, and your point of view. Climbing to the top of the real estate pyramid is hard work and personally, I would want all of the help I could get. Especially from referral partners!

CHAPTER TEN

What Is Your Real Estate Story Going To Be?

"When you have been lucky your entire life, it isn't luck."
George Schultz commenting on Ronald Reagan's political career.

Unfortunately many people are so frightened of failure that they never really get started in their real estate careers. This is why 75 percent of people who take a pre-licensing course are out of the real estate business within three years. The only things in life that you regret are the things you never try. If you are serious about achieving success in real estate, set short and long term goals. These goals should be reachable and more importantly, inspiring.

In April of 1961, cosmonaut Yuri Gagarin became the first human to be launched successfully into space. Upon his return, he became a living symbol of Russian superiority in the space race. In May, John F. Kennedy went before congress with the goal of tripling NASA's budget. He didn't suggest that the United States needed to spend more money, which he knew could be debated. Instead, he challenged congress with something inspiring, to "be the first nation to put a man on the moon, by the end of the decade". He suggested that this be a national goal, a goal that was compelling, inspiring and had a sense of urgency. In 1969, Neil Armstrong mesmerized us all by becoming the first man to walk on the surface of the moon. Everyone on the planet, with access to a television, witnessed the achievement of Kennedy's goal as it happened.

My favorite thing to do at Network Communications is to attend trade shows where I talk to real estate agents. I love to hear the clever ways they brand and network themselves and their inspirational stories. We create free networking/presentation folders for offices, teams and occasionally for individual agents. In order to do them for an individual agent, they must be a Super-agent or a

Twenty-percenter. We need to be sure that the folder advertisers receive value for their investment. It has to be economically viable for everyone. I usually know if we can work with an agent in a minute or two by asking a few simple questions.

I was recently at a state convention that had about 500 Realtors in attendance. A woman stopped by my booth and was looking at the samples on my table. She was asking me questions but with 500 people all speaking at the same time, I was having trouble hearing her. She spoke with a thick Slavic accent, in a very soft voice. I am guessing she was in her late twenty's. She was interested in an individual agent folder. I was certain she wouldn't qualify for one; she was too new, too young and hard to understand. But I noticed real intensity in her eyes, so I asked her to come back later. At least then I would be able to understand her questions, and I could ask her my qualifiers.

Her name is Georgiana, and she grew up in Romania. When she was in her early twenties, she came to Maine on a seasonal workers permit to waitress at a seaside resort. During the course of the summer, she made herself invaluable to the management and went from waitressing to supervising to working in the office. She ordered food, did payroll and managed the accounts payable. All these skills she learned on the job as she has never attended college nor has any formal training. In telling me her story, she refers to herself as an "incredibly lucky person."

The resort eventually sponsored her for a green card so she could stay on and work during the off season when only a handful of employees remain on the payroll. She spent the next two summers in Maine and would likely be there still had she not met her future husband who was vacationing with his parents. He is a software engineer from Massachusetts, so it was goodbye Maine and hello Boston. Within a year she had her first child, followed 18 months later by child number two. During the process of searching for a home in the suburbs she decided to "get in" to real estate.

After passing her licensing exam on her second try, she began her career by pushing a double stroller around town knocking on doors. I can easily imagine her asking everyone she met if they, or anyone they knew, were interested in buying or selling a home. When her children were in pre-school, she bought a car and began dropping in on expired listings. In her second year, she achieved her goal of twenty transactions and recently upped it to thirty-five. She is bringing home more money each month than her well paid and well educated husband. On her personal website, she has twenty-seven listings. During my twenty minute conversation, she used the word "lucky" to describe herself several times. Her near-term goal is to pay for her younger sister to attend college in the United States. It is a goal that I would certainly describe as inspirational. She will certainly achieve it.

By the time I met Georgiana, I had already completed this book. It was to end at Chapter 9. But I felt her story so compelling that I wanted to include it. Here is a soft spoken woman with a thick accent who managed to find life at the top of the Real Estate Pyramid in under three years. Much of the time, bringing along an infant and a toddler. Her best explanation for her success is that she is lucky. So, instead of inserting her story somewhere in the existing chapters, I leave you with it. We all know that luck had nothing to do with it. Life at the top of the Real Estate Pyramid has room for everyone with the will to get there.

Richard Latour

If you have an interesting Real estate story to share please send it to me. I may want to include it in a future edition of this book.

Rlatour@FreeFolders.com

The Real Estate Pyramid - About the Author

In the interest of full disclosure, I do not sell real estate. My background is advertising sales. I came about writing this in a circuitous manner. I spent over twenty years in business to business magazine publishing. First in sales; sales management and eventually as Associate Publisher. This specialized publishing niche was one of the original casualties of the internet. These publications are now almost entirely on-line. The scientific marketplace, which was my focus, once had over a hundred million dollars allocated to print media. Today it has less than five. Needless to say it was time for me to reinvent myself.

Like many people who get into real estate after spending years in another profession, selling houses seemed like a logical transition for me. I had always worked on a straight commission basis, a decision that resulted in a substantial financial gain to me during my career. I am not risk adverse. I operated very much like the realtors who find themselves on top of the real estate pyramid. The Twenty percenters.

I was studying for my real estate license, when I noticed an advertisement on line to be an advertising salesman. It was for a company that published presentation folders for Real Estate offices. I had never heard of this business but it was a publishing job and in my comfort zone. I was offered a straight commission job working from home and spent the next two years selling advertising to businesses in these presentation folders. The process is simple. You offer the folders to the Real Estate office at no cost. You design a cover that reflects the office and you sell advertising to local businesses who underwrite the project. The businesses network with and are selected by the office.

After two years, I started my own company. I realized that the process could be done differently and better, and I wanted to incorporate my knowledge of publishing into this format. I had noticed certain patterns in how the top agents worked, and I wanted to operate in their comfort zone. I started to refer the agents I wanted to work with as the Twenty-percenters.

When I started my company I decided to focus exclusively on the Twenty-percenters. I did this for two reasons. First, I found these folders sold quickly. Everyone one I spoke with on these folders were excited to be part of the project. Advertisers were easy to find and the space sold easily. Secondly, I found this group exceptionally easy to work with (when I can get their attention). The Twenty Percenters are accessible and have almost an encyclopedic knowledge of the businesses that they refer clients to. They often recite phone numbers of their lenders, attorney's etc. from memory when creating their lists.

 I began to notice patterns in how these agents operate. I began to see similarities in how they work with their referral partners. It became clear that in trying to qualify the best agents for us to work with, I was able to quickly identify the top performers. I find that I am in the unique position of an outsider looking in, and can observe the similarities in how the top agents operate. I am able to share this insight in a way that a top agents might not want to or even recognize. These are usually hyper focused people, and sharing secrets is not part of their job description. This is the circuitous path I took to writing this book.